WORD ROOTS
BEGINNING

LEARNING THE BUILDING BLOCKS
OF BETTER SPELLING AND VOCABULARY

Series Titles
Word Roots
Beginning
A1 ▪ A2
B1 ▪ B2

Written by

Cherie A. Plant

Stephanie W. Stevens

Graphic Design by

Danielle West

Anna Allshouse

Edited by

Patricia Gray

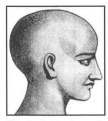

© 2008
THE CRITICAL THINKING CO.™
www.CriticalThinking.com
Phone: 800-458-4849 • Fax: 831-393-3277
P.O. Box 1610 • Seaside • CA 93955-1610
ISBN 978-1-60144-134-8

W9-AGK-999

Our book is dedicated to the children we've taught who have, in turn, taught us to be better teachers...and people.

Cherie A. Plant & Stephanie W. Stevens

About the Authors

Cherie A. Plant

A graduate in Elementary Education with a minor in Latin from the City University of New York, Cherie Plant is an accomplished etymologist (one who studies the origin and derivation of words). While teaching, Plant found that children as young as 7 years old were fascinated with decoding words such as "triskaidekaphobia" (fear of the number 13) using the knowledge of prefixes, suffixes, and root words.

Plant retired from teaching in 1995 but was convinced that other youngsters could benefit from such study. She has since devoted her time to writing language materials for all age groups, based on the study of Latin and Greek roots.

Plant now resides in Delta, Colorado. She and co-author Stephanie Stevens plan to continue writing together in the future.

Stephanie W. Stevens

Stephanie W. Stevens enjoyed early careers in advertising/public relations, and has established and directed education-related nonprofit corporations. Returning to university studies at age 45, she added to her B.A. in Art Education/Psychology by earning two Masters degrees: Education and Reading Specialist.

After years of teaching literacy—from primary grades through adult education, Stevens joined The Critical Thinking Co.™ as an editor. She then achieved a lifelong dream by becoming an author of books for children.

Stevens has a home on the Oregon coast from which she continues to edit and write for The Critical Thinking Co.™ via her Macintosh laptop.

Table of Contents

INTRODUCTION

Roots can be words, and they are also sometimes parts of words that have meanings all their own. They're hundreds of years old, having begun their lives (etymology) in the Latin and the Greek languages.

We add letters, or other word parts, in front (prefixes), or at the end (suffixes), of a root to form new words.

Let's look at the root *mar*, which means "sea". If we place the prefix "sub-" in front of the root *mar*, and the suffix "-ine" after the root, we now have the word *submarine*. Does it surprise you that a submarine is a ship that goes under the sea ?

Roots can help you understand unfamiliar words. In this book, you'll learn some easy roots and lots of words they help make.

Teaching Suggestions - For the Parent or Teacher

Word Roots Beginning is targeted for children learning at the second through fourth grade levels. The writing, or text, will likely be difficult for your child to read. If that is the case, we suggest you read the text to your child and help him or her complete each activity. These activities are designed to stimulate critical thinking, word recognition, and comprehension.

Our goal is to introduce roots as meaningful parts of many multi-syllabic words in the English language. The first 3 activities serve specifically to illustrate how roots, prefixes, and suffixes work together. Each activity becomes progressively more challenging as your child delves further into the book.

We've simplified the concept of roots as a means of introducing it to the beginner. Sometimes it may seem as if the root meaning doesn't clearly transfer to the new word. Our ever-changing language is the reason for that. Below are five basic points to remember in the study of roots:

1. Sometimes, two roots together make a word as in the word *photograph*.

2. Often, when a word ends with a root, an e or a y is added at the end, as in the words *bicycle* or *symphony*.

3. In some English words, connecting vowels and/or consonants are used to join word parts. Examples: sens + *it* + ive = *sensitive*.

4. In many English words, you will find a "combining form" (which simply means a word part which makes up the first half of a compound word). In this book we will indicate when a combining form is used as a prefix. Some examples of this are: tele, auto, and micro.

5. Some prefixes (for example, il-, im-, in-, ir-) change meaning depending on the word in which they're used. For example, in the word *invert*, the in- means "in or into." In the word *inactive*, in- means "not." Some suffixes also change meaning depending on the word's part of speech (noun, adjective, etc.). For example, in the word *graduate*, -ate means "one who, that which" when the word is used as a noun, or -ate means "to make, to act" when *graduate* is used as a verb.

Activities for practice, reinforcement, and comprehension are included with each root introduced. You'll find the answers listed in the back of this book.

****

Note: The *Word Roots* books published by The Critical Thinking Co.™ build on the basic concepts presented in this book. We suggest that you follow them in order to challenge and teach your child the full range of roots, prefixes, and suffixes, from both the Latin and Greek languages.

Lesson 1-Roots

Prefix	Meaning
micro-*	small
peri-	around, surrounding
tele-*	distance, from afar

*These are combining forms used as prefixes.

scope** — look at, examine

Plants are not the only things that grow from roots…so do words!

For example, let's start with the root, **scop**, meaning "to look at or to examine." Words or letter groups can be added to this root to grow new words.

Often, when a word ends with a root, an e or a y is added at the end, as in the words *telephone* and *euphony*. This added letter doesn't change the actual meaning of the word.

Some roots can stand on their own as a word. An example of this is the root *meter*, which means "measure." By adding beginnings (prefixes) or endings (suffixes) to roots, you form different words—with different meanings!

In the examples below, we have placed the prefixes from the chart above in front of the root **scop** to form new words.

Activity A
Draw a line from each word to the picture which shows its meaning.

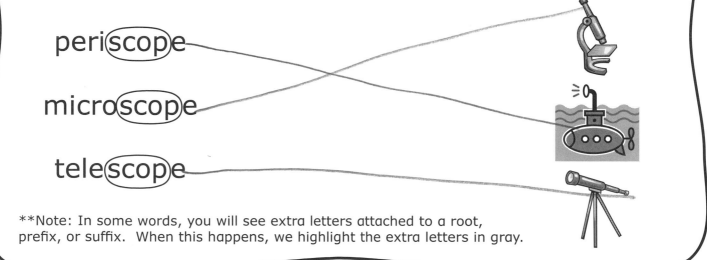

peri⟨scop⟩e

micro⟨scop⟩e

tele⟨scop⟩e

**Note: In some words, you will see extra letters attached to a root, prefix, or suffix. When this happens, we highlight the extra letters in gray.

1

Lesson 1-Roots

Activity B

Underline the prefixes and circle the roots in the choice box below. Then write the correct word at the end of its matching definition.

> periscope   microscope   telescope

1. Attached to a submarine under water, this sticks up to look for other boats: _periscope_

2. This helps see things that are far away, such as a bird high in a tree or the moon: _telescope_

3. Even the hairs on a fly's leg can be seen closely with this: _microscope_

Activity C

Some roots can go together to form new words.

ROOT   +   ROOT   =   NEW WORD

Example

hydro   +   phobia   =   hydrophobia
(water)   (fear of)   (fear of water)

> When animals have hydrophobia, better known as rabies, they have a terrifying fear of water.

Lesson 1–Roots

Here are two lists of roots. Combine a root from each list to make a new word. Write down the word next to what it means. Check a dictionary to see if you're right!

Root	Meaning
acro	height, top
astro	star, heavens
geo	earth, ground
thermo	heat

Root	Meaning
graphy	to write
meter	measure
naut	sailor, ship
phobia	fear of

New Word	Meaning
acrophobia	fear of height
astronaut	star sailor
thermometer	measure of heat
geography	writing about the earth

Activity D

Below are sentences that use four of the root combinations from Activity C. Fill in the blanks to complete the sentences.

1. _geography_ is one of my favorite subjects in school.

2. Our outside _thermometer_ reads 105 degrees!

3. Sammy's _acrophobia_ kept him from climbing the mountain.

4. The _astronaut_ circled Earth in his spacecraft.

Lesson 2–Prefixes

When letters are added to the front of a word, they're called a **prefix**. A prefix changes the meaning of a word or root.

PREFIX-   +   WORD   =   NEW WORD

Example
Uni- means "one." Put it in front of **corn**, which refers to "horn."

Prefix	Root
uni-	**corn**

Now, fill in the blank with the new word!

A ___Unicorn___ has just a single horn.

There are hundreds of prefixes! Let's begin with three of the most common.

dis- = "apart, opposite of." Put it in front of *approve* and it means "the opposite of approve," or "not approve."

re- = "again, back." Put it in front of *fry* and it means "fry again."

un- = "not." Put it in front of *hurt* and it means "not hurt."

Lesson 2–Prefixes

Activity A

Below are some words that use the prefixes from the previous page. Underline the prefix and circle the root in each word listed below. Then draw a line from each word to the picture that shows its meaning.

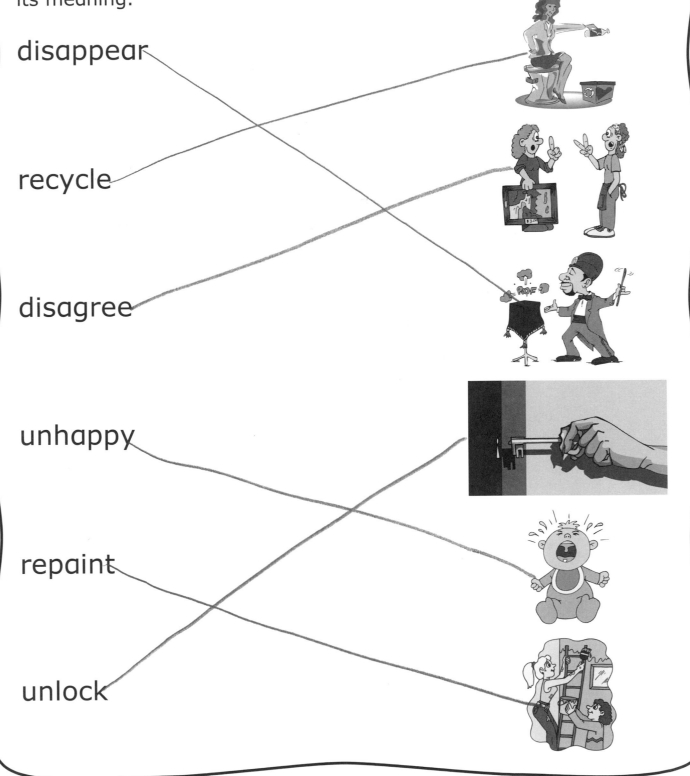

disappear

recycle

disagree

unhappy

repaint

unlock

Lesson 2–Prefixes

Activity B
Underline each prefix below and, in your own words, write what each word means.

<u>dis</u>appear _____ *not there anymore* _____

<u>re</u>cycle _____ reusible _____

<u>dis</u>agree _____ not agreing _____

<u>un</u>happy _____ not happy _____

repaint _____ Paint agian _____

unlock _____ Open the door _____

Lesson 2–Prefixes

Activity C

Underline the prefixes and circle the roots of each word in the choice box. Then use each word only once to complete the story.

disappear   recycle   disagree
unhappy   repaint   unlock   reappear

The Snake That Chose the Paint

John's grandfather had a garage full of stuff he planned to ___recycle___ or use up. One day, John and his grandfather found several half-used gallons of paint from other jobs. They decided to ___repaint___ the tool shed. They found the key to ___unlock___ the shed door and walked inside.

They looked at all the nearly full cans and couldn't decide on one color. Grandfather liked a vivid purple he saw on a back shelf. John found two cans with blue paint stains on them. They continued to ___disagree___ on what color to paint the shed and were very ___unhappy___.

As he was reaching for the purple paint can, grandfather saw a large green snake ___disappear___ behind a can. Then he watched it ___reappear___, wrapped around the can of purple paint.

"Guess I DO like that blue after all," he told John. And that's why the tool shed is now blue.

> There are at least **six** prefixes that mean "NOT." They are:
> **un-** unfed   **im-** impolite   **il-** illegal
> **a-** amoral   **in-** inability   **ir-** irrational
> Each prefix only goes with certain words. For example, *unfed* can't be *irfed*, or *afed*, or *imfed*. Most of the time, if it sounds right to you, it's correct, but you should check unfamiliar words in the dictionary.

Lesson 3–Suffixes

Now that you understand what a **prefix** is, learning about the other end of the word is easy! When letters are added to the end of a root, they're called a **suffix**.

Activity A

The most common suffixes are -**s** and -**es**. If there's more than one CAT, you add an -**s**. Now you have CATS!

Root	Meaning		Suffix	Meaning		Combined	Meaning
act	to do	+	**-ive**	one who, that which, tending to	=	**active**	being in physical motion; doing
dent	tooth	+	**-ist**	one who (works with or uses)	=	**dentist**	one who works with or treats teeth
ego	I or self	+	**-ism**	state of being, a quality or act	=	**egoism**	state of being excessively self-interested

1. The root **capt** means "to take." What then, does *captive* mean?

   Captive means to keep a person lock or
   never to let out.

2. The root **pharmac** means "drug." What then, is a *pharmacist*?

   A pharmacist deals with drugs

3. The root **centr** means "center." What then, does *centrism* mean?

   Centrism means to revol around

Lesson 3—Suffixes

Activity B
Use the chart on the previous page to help you find the meaning of each word. Then circle those words that are (people) and underline those that are a belief or a state of being.

terrorist

terrorism

journalism

journalist

egoist

egoism

optimism

optimist

hypnotist

hypnotism

idealist

idealism

plagiarism

plagiarist

modernist

modernism

Lesson 3—Suffixes

Activity C

Below are some more common suffixes that are used at the end of roots.

Suffix	Meaning	Suffix	Meaning
-able	able to be	**-ly** or **-y**	in the manner of
-er	one who, that which	**-ness**	state of being
-ful	full of		

Underline the suffix and circle the roots in the choice box words below.

teacher	golfer	quieter
teachable	acceptable	quietly
darkness	quietness	thoughtful

Using words from the choice box, choose the best word for each sentence and write it in the space. Use each word only once.

1. The students worked ___quietly___ on the project.

2. The dog was very ___acceptable___ and learned quickly.

3. Carlos was a devoted ___golfer___ and golfed every day.

4. Joy loved the library because of its ___quietness___.

5. My friend is a quiet and ___thoughtful___ person.

6. It was hard to pick a gift that was ___teachable___ to a teenager.

7. The ___darkness___ of the night helped us see the stars.

8. The classroom became ___quieter___ when our ___teacher___ handed out the test.

Lesson 4–Prefixes and Roots

Prefix	Meaning
uni–	one
bi–	two
tri–	three

Root	Meaning
cycle	circle

Activity A

Use the words in the choice box to write the name of each "cycle" beneath its picture.

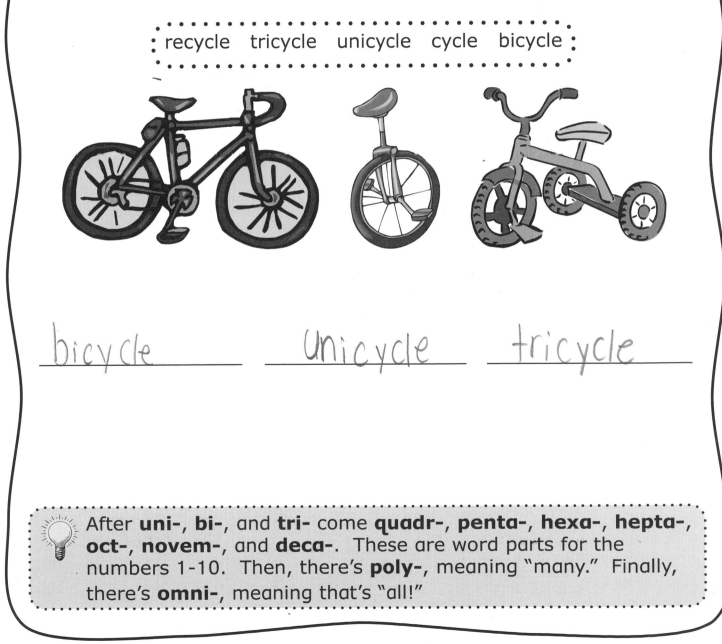

recycle   tricycle   unicycle   cycle   bicycle

bicycle   unicycle   tricycle

After **uni-**, **bi-**, and **tri-** come **quadr-**, **penta-**, **hexa-**, **hepta-**, **oct-**, **novem-**, and **deca-**. These are word parts for the numbers 1-10. Then, there's **poly-**, meaning "many." Finally, there's **omni-**, meaning that's "all!"

Lesson 4–Prefixes and Roots

Activity B

The root **cycle** can also mean a constantly repeating series of events or processes.

A "life cycle" is one example.

To the right is the life cycle of a frog.

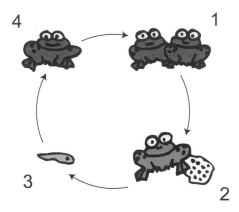

1. The cycle starts with a female and a male frog.
2. The female lays eggs.
3. The eggs hatch into tadpoles.
4. The tadpoles grow into male and female frogs, so the cycle continues.

Now, number the life cycle of a tomato plant! Put a number from 1-4 beside each image to show where it would belong in the cycle.

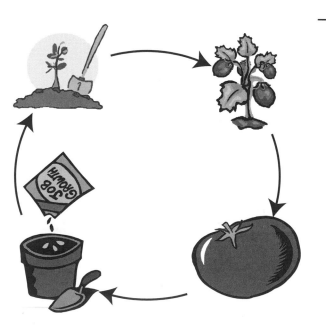

Lesson 5–Prefixes and Roots

Prefix*	Meaning
micro-	small
tele-	from afar, distance
xylo-	wood

Root	Meaning
phone	sound

*These are combining forms used as prefixes.

Activity A

Underline the prefixes and circle the roots in the words below. Then draw a line from each word to the picture which shows its meaning.

telephone

xylophone

microphone

Activity B

The words above have been formed by combining the above prefixes with the root **phone**. Write the correct word for each definition below.

1. An instrument used to make small sounds loud: _____

2. An instrument that sends sounds and speech over distances: _____

3. A musical instrument with different-sized bars that are struck with a small, wooden hammer to make musical sounds: _____

Lesson 5–Prefixes and Roots

Activity C
Phon is used in other interesting words. The **prefixes** listed below can all be used with the root **phon.**

Prefix	Meaning
eu-*	good, well, pleasant
hydro-	water
mega-*	large, great
sym-	with, together

Root	Meaning
phone or y	sound
opto	eye, vision

*These are combining forms used as prefixes.

Underline the prefixes and circle the root in the choice box words below. Then write the correct word for each definition.

> symphony   euphony   optophone
> hydrophone   megaphone

1. A cone-shaped device used to make a voice sound louder: _____

2. A pleasant sound: _____

3. A device that turns writing into sounds (used by blind people): _____

4. A receiver for listening to sound through water: _____

5. A variety of sounds played together: _____

💡 What about "saxophone"? The word "saxophone" looks like a root word combination, but it isn't. The root **sax** means "rock" and that doesn't make sense when combined with the root **phone**. Adolphe Sax, a Belgium inventor, designed the saxophone and introduced it to the world in 1841. It's named for him!

Lesson 6–Prefixes and Roots

Prefix	Meaning
ab-	away, from
dis-	apart, opposite of
e-	out, away, from
inter -	between, among

Root	Meaning
rupt	to break

Activity A

Underline the prefixes and circle the roots in the choice box words. Then write the correct word for each definition.

disrupt   erupt   interrupt   abrupt

1. To break apart or into an activity causing confusion or disorder: _____

2. To come between or break into an activity or conversation: _____

3. To break out of or burst from; explode: _____

4. Broken away or from something without warning: _____

Lesson 6–Prefixes and Roots

Activity B

Each sentence uses one of the two words in the choice box below. Write the correct word in each sentence. Then, under each picture, write the number of the sentence that matches the picture.

:··:
:   abrupt   or   erupted   :
:··:

1. The pigs almost walked over the _____ cliff edge.

2. Sally's face _____ into a red rash.

3. The water pipe broke and water _____ forcefully.

4. He screeched to an _____ stop just in front of the ball.

5. The volcano _____ and hot lava poured out.

6. The car stopped at the _____ end of the mountain road.

Lesson 6–Prefixes and Roots

interrupt or disrupted

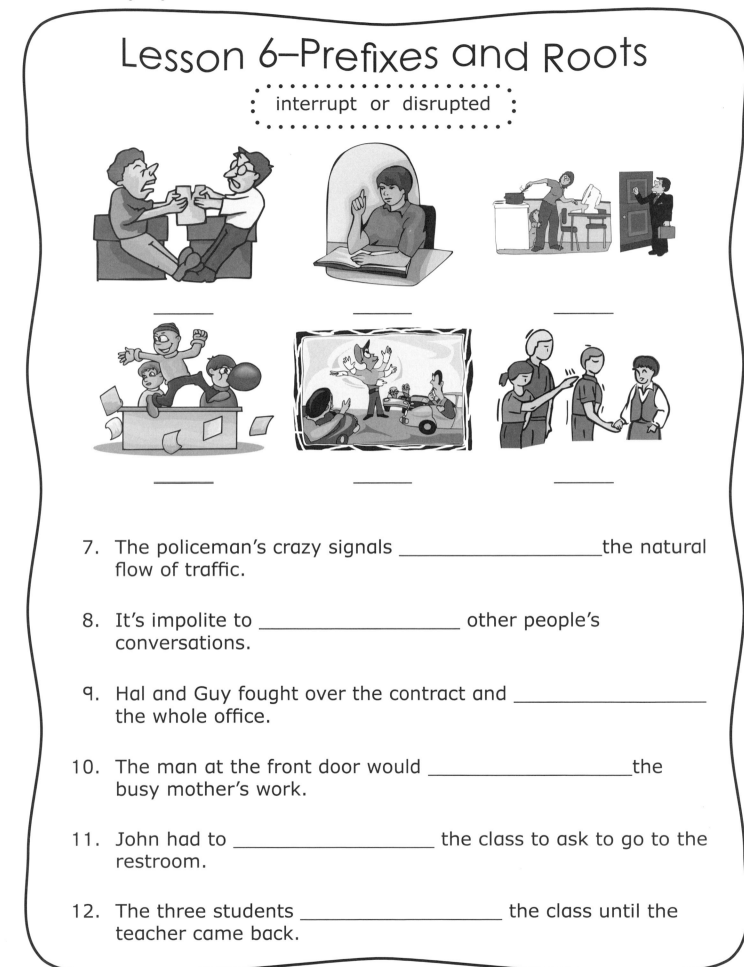

7. The policeman's crazy signals _____the natural flow of traffic.

8. It's impolite to _____ other people's conversations.

9. Hal and Guy fought over the contract and _____ the whole office.

10. The man at the front door would _____the busy mother's work.

11. John had to _____ the class to ask to go to the restroom.

12. The three students _____ the class until the teacher came back.

Lesson 7–Prefixes and Roots

Prefix	Meaning
counter-	against, opposite
inter-	between, among
re-	back, again
trans -	through, across, beyond

Root	Meaning
act	to do, to drive

Activity A

Underline the prefixes and circle the roots in the choice box below. Then write the correct word for each definition.

react   transact   interact   counteract

1. To do or act against something: _____

2. To respond to something (by an action or show of feelings): _____

3. To do things or talk with others: _____

4. To do business with people or companies: _____

Lesson 7–Prefixes and Roots

Activity B
Underline the prefix and circle the root in each word listed below. Then circle the picture that best illustrates the word.

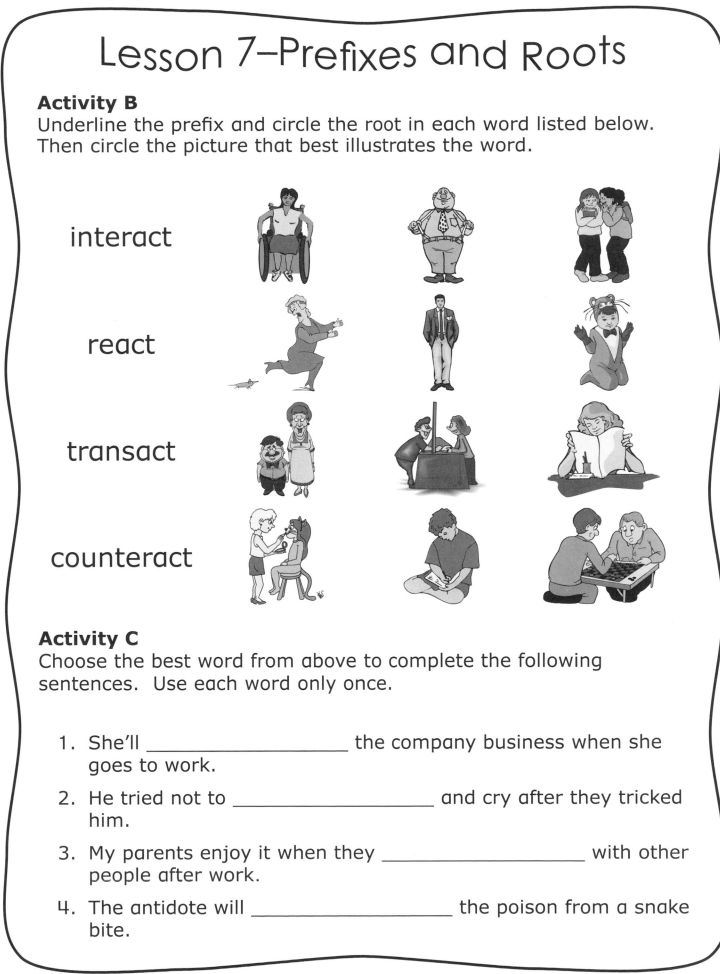

interact

react

transact

counteract

Activity C
Choose the best word from above to complete the following sentences. Use each word only once.

1. She'll _____ the company business when she goes to work.

2. He tried not to _____ and cry after they tricked him.

3. My parents enjoy it when they _____ with other people after work.

4. The antidote will _____ the poison from a snake bite.

Lesson 8–Roots and Suffixes

Root	Meaning
loc	place

Suffix	Meaning
-al	like, related to
-ale	place where
-ate	to make, to act
-ly	in the manner of

Activity A

Underline the suffixes and circle the roots in the choice box below.*
Then write the correct word for each definition.

> locate   local   locale   locally

1. A place or area where something
    special was, is, or happened: _____

2. Like or related to a particular
    place: _____

3. To find where something is: _____

4. In the manner of being local (in a
    particular place or area): _____

*Note: a word can have more than one suffix.

Lesson 8–Roots and Suffixes

Activity B
Circle each item that would help you locate a place.

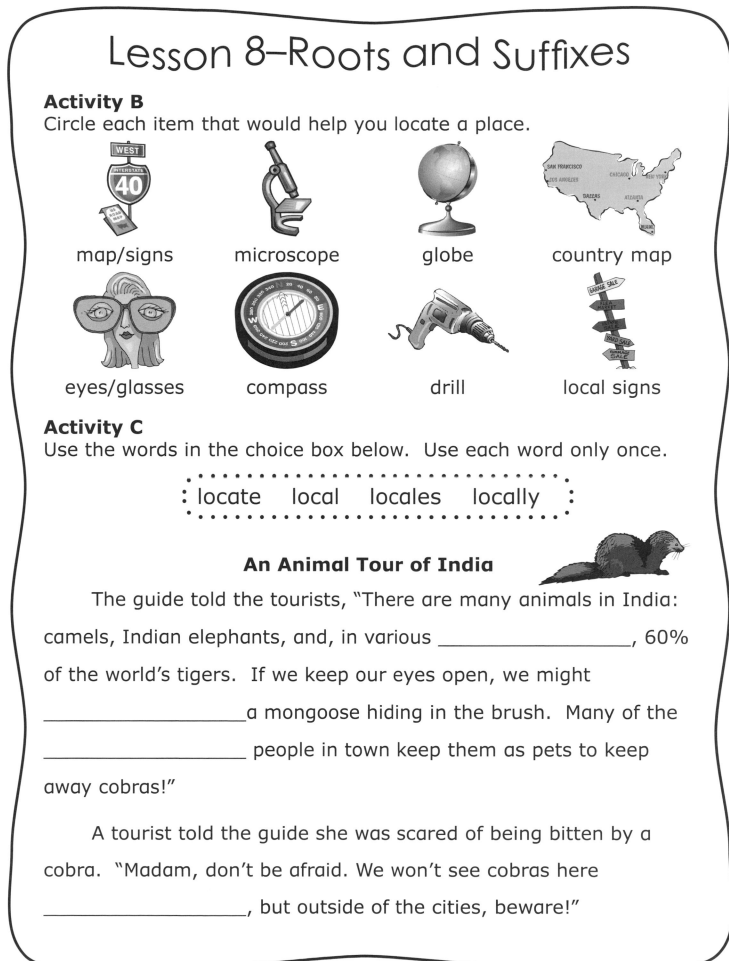

map/signs   microscope   globe   country map

eyes/glasses   compass   drill   local signs

Activity C
Use the words in the choice box below. Use each word only once.

locate   local   locales   locally

An Animal Tour of India

The guide told the tourists, "There are many animals in India: camels, Indian elephants, and, in various _____, 60% of the world's tigers. If we keep our eyes open, we might _____ a mongoose hiding in the brush. Many of the _____ people in town keep them as pets to keep away cobras!"

A tourist told the guide she was scared of being bitten by a cobra. "Madam, don't be afraid. We won't see cobras here _____, but outside of the cities, beware!"

Lesson 9—Roots and Suffixes

Root	Meaning	Suffix	Meaning
medi	half, middle, halfway between	-an	like, related to
		-ate	to make, to act
		at-or	one who, that which
		-um	of or belonging to

Activity A

Underline the suffixes and circle the roots in the choice box below. Then write the correct word for each definition.

: mediate   medium   median   mediator :

1. To act or come between two opposite sides to solve a problem: _____

2. One who acts between two opposite sides to solve a problem: _____

3. Of a middle size, amount, or quality; not large nor small: _____

4. Something that is related to or in the middle: _____

The word *mediocre* is from two roots: **medi** and **ocris**, which means "stony mountain." It originally meant "going only halfway up the mountain." The use of this word has evolved over time to mean something done "half as good as is possible." This is an excellent example of word etymology.

Lesson 9—Roots and Suffixes

Activity B

Draw a line from each word in the choice box to the picture which best illustrates it.

: mediate   medium   median   mediator :

Activity C

Underline the suffixes and circle the roots in the choice box above. Then use each word just once to complete the story.

An Article From the Gazette

The weedy _____ in our small town

goes right down the middle of Main Street. Old Mrs. Ringo planted

bright flowers and kept up the _____-sized bushes,

trees, and ferns. When she was unable to do it anymore, three

groups in town each thought they should take over. Our own Chu

Ying spoke to the town council about the problem. The council voted

to have the garden club two towns over _____ the

issue.

Amazingly, the _____ solved the issue quickly.

Everyone was pleased, even the flowers—but especially Chu, who is

just nine years old!

Lesson 10–Roots and Suffixes

Root	Meaning
grad	step

Suffix	Meaning
u-al	like, related to
u-ate	one who, that which
u-ation	an action or process
i-ent	like, related to

Activity A

Underline the suffixes and circle the roots in the choice box below. Then write the correct word for each definition.

gradual   gradient   graduate   graduation

1. An action or activity that happens when steps of study are successfully finished, such as high school or college: _____

2. Related to steps of change in something, such as a change in color (rainbow), temperature, or when a road goes higher or lower: _____

3. One who has finished each grade or step in high school, college, or other program of study: _____

4. Relating to small steps of change in something: _____

A *gradient* in color is when two or more colors blend together. Here is a simple example of a gradient, beginning with white and ending with black.

Lesson 10–Roots and Suffixes

Activity B
Underline the suffixes and circle the roots in the choice box below. Then use each word only once to complete the sentences.

gradual   gradient   graduate   graduation

1. Katrina's _____ was attended by her entire family.

2. The speaker at the ceremony was a college _____.

3. There was a _____ decline in grandpa's health.

4. The _____ colors of a rainbow can be seen after a rain.

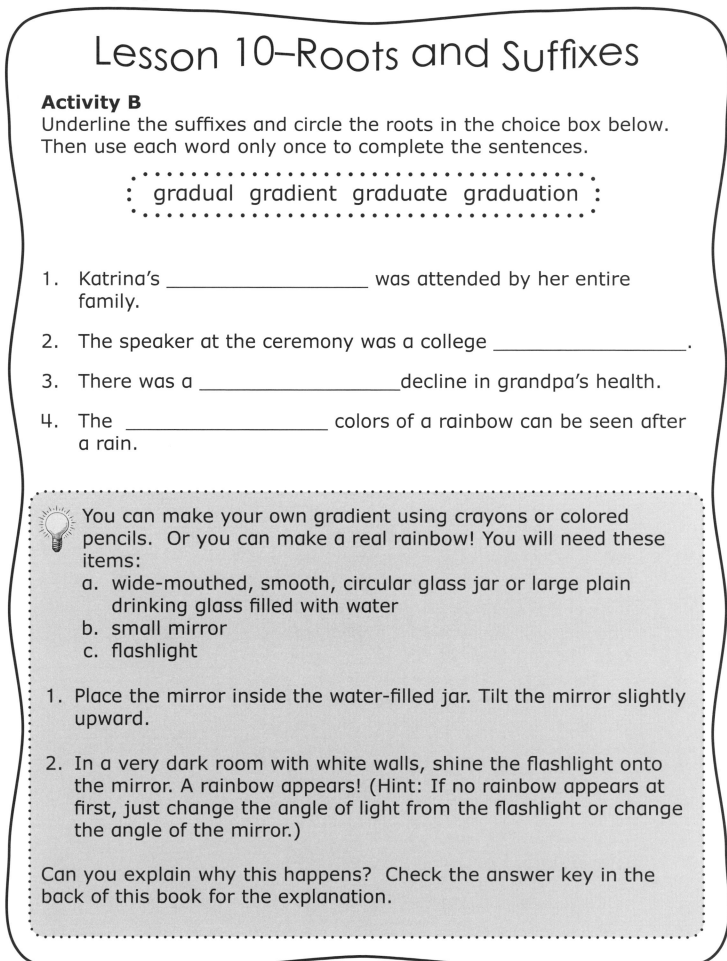 You can make your own gradient using crayons or colored pencils. Or you can make a real rainbow! You will need these items:
   a. wide-mouthed, smooth, circular glass jar or large plain drinking glass filled with water
   b. small mirror
   c. flashlight

1. Place the mirror inside the water-filled jar. Tilt the mirror slightly upward.

2. In a very dark room with white walls, shine the flashlight onto the mirror. A rainbow appears! (Hint: If no rainbow appears at first, just change the angle of light from the flashlight or change the angle of the mirror.)

Can you explain why this happens? Check the answer key in the back of this book for the explanation.

Lesson 11–Roots and Suffixes

Root	Meaning
audi	to hear

Suffix	Meaning
-ence	state, quality, act
-ist	one who
-ology	study of, science
t**-orium**	place where
t**-ory**	like, relating to
-tion	state, condition, act

Activity A

Underline the suffixes and circle the roots in the choice box below. Then write the correct word for each definition.

> auditory   audition   audiology
> auditorium   audiologist   audience

1. A place where lectures, concerts, and other events are held: _____

2. The scientific study of hearing: _____

3. A brief act of singing or performing another skill by someone applying for a role in a movie or play: _____

4. One who is trained to treat hearing and ear problems: _____

5. The state of being a group of people listening to a performance, movie, or speech: _____

6. Of or relating to the process of hearing: _____

Lesson 11—Roots and Suffixes

Activity B
Draw a line from each word to the picture that shows its meaning.

auditorium

audition

audiologist

audience

Activity C
Use words from the choice box on the previous page to complete the story below.

What? What Did You Say?

People studying _____ are concerned about the

noise in our lives—and in our ears.

Recently, students at our school gathered in the school

_____ to learn about noises. Suddenly, we

were hearing chainsaws, snowmobiles, and even car horns.

The speaker, an _____, told us that all those

sounds were over 100 decibels in sound measurement. Even sounds

coming through ear buds to an _____ of one person

can be over 100 decibels! The safest level for our ears is under 85

decibels.

Hearing high _____ levels can cause

permanent damage to our ears.

Show What You Know

Review A

Part 1 Write the number of the correct meaning in the space following each prefix.

Prefix	Word		Meaning
ab-	abrupt	_10_	1. apart, opposite of
bi-	bicycle	_12_	2. again, back
counter-	counteract	_____	3. out, away, from
dis-	disrupt	_____	4. not
e-	erupt	_____	5. good, well, pleasant
eu-	euphony	_____	6. through, across, beyond
inter-	interrupt	_____	7. large, great
mega-	megaphone	_____	8. one
micro-	microphone	_____	9. with, together
re-	repaint	_____	10. away, from
sym-	symphony	_____	11. small
trans-	transact	_____	12. two
tri-	tricycle	_____	13. between, among
un-	unhappy	_____	14. against, opposite
uni-	unicorn	_____	15. three

Show What You Know

Part 2
Only one of the prefixes below is correct for the root. Underline the one you think is correct, then write the new word.

Prefix	Root	New Word
1. <u>re-</u> / ab- / un-	cycle	recycle
2. <u>un-</u> / eu- / pre-	lock	unlock
3. uni- / sym- / bi-	corn	_____
4. ab- / dis- / un-	agree	_____
5. pre- / dis- / ab-	appear	_____
6. ab- / inter- / bi-	act	_____
7. bi- / mega- / re-	phone	_____
8. un- / bi- / trans-	happy	_____
9. re- / bi- / un-	paint	_____
10. trans- / tri- / e-	cycle	_____
11. bi- / counter- / un-	act	_____
12. e- / un- / tri-	rupt	_____
13. ab- / inter- / sym-	phony	_____
14. un- / dis- / bi-	approve	_____
15. uni- / micro- / trans-	scope	_____

Show What You Know

Part 3

In your own words*, write the word and the meaning of the combinations you made on the previous page.

<u>Word</u>   <u>Meaning</u>

1. _____   _____

                                    _____

2. _____   _____

                                    _____

3. _____   _____

                                    _____

4. _____   _____

                                    _____

5. _____   _____

                                    _____

6. _____   _____

                                    _____

7. _____   _____

*Note: Any reasonably correct wording is acceptable.

Show What You Know

Word	Meaning
8. _____	_____
	_____
9. _____	_____
	_____
10. _____	_____
	_____
11. _____	_____
	_____
12. _____	_____
	_____
13. _____	_____
	_____
14. _____	_____
	_____
15. _____	_____
	_____

Show What You Know

Review B

Part 1

Only one of the suffixes is correct for the root below. Underline the one you think is correct, then write the new word.

Root	Suffix	New Word
1. medi	-um / i-ent / -ology	*medium*
2. grad	-ly / u-ate / -ist	_____
3. loc	-able / -ism / -ale	_____
4. audi	t-orium / at-or / t-ist	_____
5. grad	i-ent / -ology / at-or	_____
6. medi	-ly / at-or / -orium	_____
7. audi	t-ion / t-ate / t-ly	_____
8. loc	-ual / -ate / i-ent	_____

Part 2

Using your own words, write the word and the meaning of the combinations you made.

Word	Meaning
1. _____	_____
	_____
2. _____	_____
	_____
3. _____	_____
	_____

Show What You Know

Word   Meaning

4. _____   _____

   _____

5. _____   _____

   _____

6. _____   _____

   _____

   _____

7. _____   _____

   _____

   _____

8. _____   _____

   _____

*Note: Any reasonably correct wording is acceptable.

Review C

Below are both review and new words that have a prefix and a suffix added to a root. Circle the roots and underline the prefixes and suffixes.

Example   re (place) able

recyclable   inflexible

interaction   transportation

removable   interference

construction   convertible

eruption   retractable

revival

Lesson 12–Prefixes, Roots, and Suffixes

Prefix	Meaning
e-	out, away, from
pre-	before

Root

dict

say, speak

Suffix	Meaning
-ary	that which
-ate	to make, to act
-ion	an action or process

Activity A

Underline the prefixes and suffixes and circle the roots in the choice box below. Then write the correct word for each definition.

> predict   prediction   diction
> edict   dictionary   dictate

1. A reference book that contains an alphabetical list of words with information about them: _____

2. A public statement from an official (usually government related): _____

3. The process or manner in which one speaks: _____

4. A statement of what a person or group thinks will happen before it actually does: _____

5. To speak as one in complete authority, making rules and decisions for others to follow: _____

6. To say that a thing will happen before it actually does: _____

Lesson 12–Prefixes, Roots, and Suffixes

Activity B
Write the correct word to complete the sentences below.

1. The weatherman failed to make the _____ that a
   snowstorm would ruin our picnic plans. *edict-prediction*

2. Before his speech, Liam practiced his _____.
   diction-dictate

3. A _____ is the best source for accurate meanings
   prediction-dictionary
   of words.

4. The _____ proclaimed by the leader required that
   prediction-edict
   all women cover their faces.

5. One can never _____ what a clown will do.
   predict-edict

6. Jan is so bossy she wants to _____ rules for the
   dictate-predict
   class to follow.

7. If you don't use good _____, your phone
   dictionary-diction
   messages could sound garbled.

8. A _____ provides valuable information about
   dictionary-prediction
   word pronunciations.

9. Long ago, a king would give an _____ that his
   prediction-edict
   countrymen had to follow.

10. Kyle tried to _____ that his school's soccer team
    predict-dictate
    would win the final game.

11. It's uncanny, but Danielle's _____ actually came
    diction-prediction
    true.

12. "You can't _____ what I can or can't do," Haley
    dictate-predict
    told her mother angrily.

Lesson 12–Prefixes, Roots, and Suffixes

Activity C
Choose the best word from the choice box below to complete each sentence and write it in the space.

> predict   prediction   diction
> edict   dictionary   dictate

1. Scientists _____ that global warming will change our planet.

2. Contestants were judged on both their _____ and speech content.

3. In the 15th century, a Japanese government _____ prohibited people from wearing gold or silver bracelets.

4. The conqueror was the only one who could _____ the terms of surrender.

5. The actor was told to improve his _____.

6. We always use a _____ when we play *Scrabble*.

7. We didn't believe the weatherman's _____ that a blizzard was heading our way.

8. I _____ that it will rain tomorrow.

9. The child tried to _____ to his parents what he wanted to do.

10. The dictator's _____ forbids speaking against the regime.

11. The teacher told Lana to look the word up in the _____.

12. Don't ask me to make a _____ about tomorrow's meeting.

Lesson 12–Prefixes, Roots, and Suffixes

Activity D

Write a complete sentence for each word in the choice box below.

predict   prediction   diction
edict   dictionary   dictate

1. _____

   _____

2. _____

   _____

3. _____

   _____

4. _____

   _____

5. _____

   _____

6. _____

   _____

Lesson 13–Prefixes, Roots, and Suffixes

Prefix	Meaning
con-	with, together
in-	not
re-	back, again
trans-	across, through, beyond

Root

fer

to carry, bear, produce

Suffix	Meaning
-able	able to be
-ence	state, quality act
t**-ile**	like, relating to

Activity A

Underline the prefixes and suffixes and circle the roots in the choice box below. Then write the correct word for each definition.

> confer transfer fertile
> reference infertile transferable

1. Relating to being able to produce crops or offspring: _____

2. To carry across from one place to another: _____

3. A source to back up or produce authoritative facts: _____

4. To talk with another person or persons in order to produce a decision: _____

5. Relating to not able to produce crops or offspring: _____

6. Able to be carried across from one place to another: _____

Lesson 13–Prefixes, Roots, and Suffixes

Activity B

Write the correct word to complete the sentences below.

1. Charlie needed to _____ with his banker before deciding to sell. *confer-transfer*

2. Unfortunately, his source of _____ was an outdated book. *transfer-reference*

3. The airline ticket was not _____ to another individual. *fertile-transferable*

4. If the panda is _____, she might produce a baby *fertile-infertile*

   panda, but this rarely happens in a zoo.

5. Let's _____ these files to the new cabinets. *confer-transter*

6. The two lawyers decided to _____ on the best way to handle the case. *transfer-confer*

7. Anything will grow in this rich, _____ ground. *fertile-infertile*

8. Our library has an entire floor of _____ materials. *transferable-reference*

9. The garden soil was dry and _____. *fertile-infertile*

10. The _____ of the ship's cargo onto the pier was *transfer-reference*

    halted by a severe storm.

11. The poor farmers were trying to grow crops on _____ soil. *fertile-infertile*

12. The form clearly stated the item was not _____ to another party. *transferable-fertile*

Lesson 13–Prefixes, Roots, and Suffixes

Activity C

Choose the best word from the choice box below to complete each sentence and write it in the space.

> confer   transfer   fertile
> reference   infertile   transferable

1. The prisoner wanted to _____ with his lawyer before pleading guilty.

2. We were surprised that the old mare was still _____.

3. The passengers were asked to _____ from one bus to another.

4. We turned to the _____ section of the book to find the answers.

5. Dad found that the car title was _____ to the new owner.

6. This year's drought was the cause of the soil being

   _____.

7. Prior to the game, the football team had to _____ with their coach.

8. After his sophomore year, Al decided to _____ to another university.

9. Ownership of the property was _____ to Ted's wife.

10. The solution to their problem was the result of Kevin's

    _____ mind.

11. The internet is a popular source of _____.

12. The breeders were disappointed to find their registered border

    collie was _____.

Lesson 13–Prefixes, Roots, and Suffixes

Activity D
Write a complete sentence for each word in the choice box below.

> confer   transfer   fertile
> reference   infertile   transferable

1. _____

_____

2. _____

_____

3. _____

_____

4. _____

_____

5. _____

_____

6. _____

_____

Lesson 14–Prefixes, Roots, and Suffixes

Prefix	Meaning
in-	not
re-	again, back

Root

flex, flect

to bend

Suffix	Meaning
-ible	able to be
-ion	an action or process
-or	one who, that which

Activity A

Underline the prefixes and suffixes and circle the roots in the choice box below. Then write the correct word for each definition.

> flexible   inflexible   reflection
> flexor   reflex

1. A muscle that contracts back to bend a joint (like a knee or finger): _____

2. The process of bending back (an image in a mirror) or thinking back: _____

3. The state of not being able to bend or change: _____

4. An automatic bending back away from something (like fire) or reacting to something (knee jerk): _____

5. Being able to bend or change: _____

Lesson 14–Prefixes, Roots, and Suffixes

Activity B
Write the correct word to complete the sentences below.

1. The committee was _____ in its opposition to our
   request. *reflex-inflexible*

2. Craig experienced a great deal of pain when he sprained his
   _____ muscle.
   flexible-flexor

3. _____ plastic is an alternative to the more rigid
   Flexible-Inflexible
   copper piping.

4. Linda gave much _____ to the problem but still
   had no answer. *reflex-reflection*

5. When Amy poked me in the shoulder, my arm went up in a

   _____ response.
   reflex-flexible

6. Upon _____ , Jeff decided not to run for office.
   reflection-reflex

7. The quarterback could not finish the game once he pulled his

   _____ muscle.
   inflexible-flexor

8. The springs were made of _____ steel.
   reflex-flexible

9. Our high school wrestling champion is very strong and has

   amazing _____ action.
   reflex-inflexible

10. Marble is an _____ material.
    inflexible-flexor

Lesson 14–Prefixes, Roots, and Suffixes

Activity C
Choose the best word from the choice box below to complete each sentence and write it in the space.

> flexible   inflexible   reflection
> flexor   reflex

1. Upon _____, I decided I was in the wrong.

2. Rubber is a _____ substance.

3. The president has adopted an _____ position on immigration.

4. Bridget injured a _____ muscle in the car accident.

5. I didn't mean to punch you; it was just a _____ action.

6. My computer is too slow and _____ to meet my needs.

7. Dancers and gymnasts need to be very _____.

8. The statistics were a _____ on the change in people's spending habits.

9. The doctor wants Hal to have physical therapy for his sprained _____ muscle.

10. Bob was an excellent fighter pilot because he had extremely fast _____ responses.

Lesson 14–Prefixes, Roots, and Suffixes

Activity D
Write a complete sentence for each word in the choice box below.

flexible   inflexible   reflection
flexor   reflex

1. _____

   _____

2. _____

   _____

3. _____

   _____

4. _____

   _____

5. _____

   _____

Lesson 15—Prefixes, Roots, and Suffixes

Prefix	Meaning
ex-	out, away, from
im-	in, into
sup-	under, below
trans-	across, through, beyond

Root

port

to carry, bring

Suffix	Meaning
-able	able to be
-ation	an action or process

Activity A

Underline the prefixes and suffixes and circle the roots in the choice box below. Then write the correct word for each definition.

> transportation   export   import
> support   portable

1. The action or process of carrying people or goods from one place to another: _____

2. To bring goods from a foreign source into a country: _____

3. Able to be carried from one place to another: _____

4. To send goods out to another country: _____

5. The act of bearing the weight of or making stronger: _____

Lesson 15–Prefixes, Roots, and Suffixes

Activity B
Write the correct word to complete the sentences below.

1. They were hoping to _____ their entire corn crop to Japan this year.
   import-export

2. Wooden sticks make a good _____ for my tomato plants.
   support-transportation

3. The lengthy drought forced them to _____ most of their crops from Brazil.
   import-export

4. The _____ of coal is done by the railroad.
   support-transportation

5. A laptop computer is highly _____.
   portable-transportation

6. They will _____ the goods in large crates.
   support-export

7. My friends were a lot of _____ when I lost my job.
   import-support

8. We _____ a large number of automobiles from Korea.
   export-import

9. Air _____ of heavy items can be very costly.
   transportation-support

10. I have a _____ TV in my bedroom.
    support-portable

Lesson 15–Prefixes, Roots, and Suffixes

Activity C
Choose the best word from the choice box below to complete each sentence and write it in the space.

> transportation   export   import
> support   portable

1. The United States and Japan _____ huge quantities of oil from other countries.

2. Kenneth always wears a bandage to _____ his knee when jogging.

3. Our cosmetics sell so quickly here that we have no need to

   _____ them anyplace else.

4. The Alaskan pipeline was built for the _____ of oil to coastal ports.

5. After ankle surgery, Tricia used crutches to _____ her weight.

6. Our baby grand piano is not very _____.

7. We export wheat to Russia and _____ silk from Japan.

8. Dad carried the _____ kennel from the car into the house.

9. Due to poor production, India will not be able to _____ tea this year.

10. With the high cost of fuel, bicycles are a cheap means of

    _____.

Lesson 15–Prefixes, Roots, and Suffixes

Activity D
Write a complete sentence for each word in the choice box below.

transportation   export   import
support   portable

1. _____

_____

_____

2. _____

_____

_____

3. _____

_____

_____

4. _____

_____

_____

5. _____

_____

_____

Lesson 16–Prefixes, Roots, and Suffixes

Prefix	Meaning	Root		Suffix	Meaning
com-	with, together	**plen, plete**		**-ion**	an action or process
de-	from, away, down, apart	full		**t-y**	state of

Activity A

Underline the prefixes and suffixes and circle the roots in the choice box below. Then write the correct word for each definition.

> complete   deplete   plenty
> completion   depletion

1. The process of coming fully together to an expected end: _____

2. To take away from something such as supplies, resources, or energy: _____

3. Filled with or having all necessary parts together: _____

4. The state of having a full amount: _____

5. The action or process of taking away from something: _____

Lesson 16–Prefixes, Roots, and Suffixes

Activity B
Write the correct word to complete the sentences below.

1. Our car has _____ of room for everybody.
   completion-plenty

2. This year's drought will _____ our water supply.
   complete-deplete

3. The _____ of the new road is scheduled for June.
   depletion-completion

4. The library has a _____ set of Robert Louis
   Stevenson's books. *complete-deplete*

5. The country was facing the _____ of their oil
   resources. *completion-depletion*

6. We are two weeks away from the _____ of the
   school year. *completion-depletion*

7. By taking short breaks, the marathon runner was able to not
   _____ his supply of energy.
   deplete-complete

8. We allowed _____ of time to get to the airport.
   depletion-plenty

9. Our triumph was _____.
   deplete-complete

10. After two sleepless nights, I could feel the _____
    of my energy. *depletion-completion*

Lesson 16–Prefixes, Roots, and Suffixes

Activity C
Choose the best word from the choice box below to complete each sentence and write it in the space.

> complete   deplete   plenty
> completion   depletion

1. My doctor advised me to drink _____ of water everyday.

2. Many factors are leading to the _____ of the ozone layer.

3. Our teacher was unable to _____ the school year.

4. Many illnesses can _____ the body of important nutrients.

5. The _____ of the film will take four months.

6. Increased expenditures have caused a _____ of the company's funds.

7. We wear _____ of warm clothing when we go skiing.

8. The work crew will be paid upon _____ of the job.

9. If we continue to _____ our natural resources, we will assuredly damage our environment.

10. The builder should _____ our house by the end of the month.

Lesson 16—Prefixes, Roots, and Suffixes

Activity D
Write a complete sentence for each word in the choice box below.

> complete   deplete   plenty
> completion   depletion

1. _____

_____

_____

2. _____

_____

_____

3. _____

_____

_____

4. _____

_____

_____

5. _____

_____

_____

Lesson 17–Prefixes, Roots, and Suffixes

Prefix	Meaning
de-	from, away, down, apart
in-	in, into
in-	not
pre-	before

Root

scribe, script

to write

Suffix	Meaning
-able	able to be
-ion	an action or process
-ive	tending to

Activity A

Underline the prefixes and suffixes and circle the roots in the choice box below. Then write the correct word for each definition.

> script   inscribe   describe
> descriptive   indescribable   inscription

1. Not able to be understood or pictured from words alone: _____

2. The written version of something to be performed in a movie or play: _____

3. To create a picture in a person's mind from the use of words alone: _____

4. To write, print, or engrave words or letters into a surface (glass, stone, wood, or other material): _____

5. Tending to use words that tell about smell, sight, sound, texture, and taste to create a picture in a person's mind: _____

6. Words or letters written, printed, or engraved into a surface: _____

Lesson 17–Prefixes, Roots, and Suffixes

Activity B

Write the correct word to complete the sentences below.

1. The _____ on his watch read: "With love, Helen, 1968." *inscription-script*

2. The colors in the sunset were _____. *descriptive-indescribable*

3. Carrie didn't like the way the _____ for the play was written. *script-inscription*

4. The eyewitness was asked to _____ the criminal. *inscribe-describe*

5. The _____ on the gravestone was almost illegible. *script-inscription*

6. The portrait of the young girl had _____ beauty. *indescribable-descriptive*

7. Our English teacher wants us to use _____ words. *indescribable-descriptive*

8. The _____ was delivered to the director ahead of *inscription-script*

   schedule.

9. I had the jeweler _____ my children's names and *describe-inscribe*

   birthdates on my charm bracelet.

10. _____ what a triangle looks like. *Describe-Inscribe*

11. They gave very _____ details of their trip. *indescribable-descriptive*

12. Uncle Harry told Aunt Bess to be sure to _____ the *inscribe-describe*

    words, "The best is yet to come," on his tombstone.

Lesson 17–Prefixes, Roots, and Suffixes

Activity C
Choose the best word from the choice box below to complete each sentence and write it in the space.

> script   inscribe   describe
> descriptive   indescribable   inscription

1. The artistry of Michelangelo's *Pieta* is _____.

2. The _____ on the tombstone read: "I told you I was sick!"

3. Several changes were made to the movie _____.

4. Tyler wanted to _____ his initials on his belt buckle.

5. The detective gave a very _____ report of his findings.

6. I asked Tara to _____ the movie in great detail.

7. The _____ on Gina's bracelet read: "With love forever, Steve."

8. We vacationed on an island in the Pacific that had _____ beauty.

9. The _____ was performed before a live audience.

10. They could _____ only a small amount of words on their grandma's tombstone.

11. I asked the salesgirl to _____ the dress to me over the phone.

12. One of my most challenging subjects in college was _____ geometry.

Lesson 17–Prefixes, Roots, and Suffixes

Activity D

Write a complete sentence for each word in the choice box below.

> script   inscribe   describe
> descriptive   indescribable   inscription

1. _____

_____

2. _____

_____

3. _____

_____

4. _____

_____

5. _____

_____

6. _____

_____

Lesson 18–Prefixes, Roots, and Suffixes

Prefix	Meaning	Root	Suffix	Meaning
con-	with, together	**sens, sent** to feel, to perceive	**-ation**	an action or process
dis-	apart, opposite of		**it-ive**	tending to
in-	not		**i-ment**	that which

Activity A

Underline the prefixes and suffixes and circle the roots in the choice box below. Then write the correct word for each definition.

> consent   sentiment   sensitive
> sensation   insensitive   dissent

1. Tending to feel emotions and physical things easily: _____

2. Feeling it is all right to do something, giving permission, from one person to another: _____

3. That which is based on a feeling or emotion: _____

4. Tending to not respond to other people's feelings or things that happen to or around oneself: _____

5. The act of disagreeing with the feelings or opinions of others; taking an opposing point of view: _____

6. The process of feeling something physically through one's senses: _____

Lesson 18–Prefixes, Roots, and Suffixes

Activity B
Write the correct word to complete the sentences below.

1. Marla's parents gave her their _____ to bring
   home the new puppy.   *dissent-consent*

2. The students expressed much negative _____ over
   the new dress code.   *sentiment-sensation*

3. Pascal is highly _____ to comments about his
   short stature.   *insensitive-sensitive*

4. The medication caused a numbing _____ in Gina's
   arm.   *sensation-sentiment*

5. Selfish people tend to be _____ to the needs of
   others.   *insensitive-sensitive*

6. The governor was concerned over the _____
   among his people.   *consent-dissent*

7. The author gave her _____ to make a film from
   her book.   *consent-dissent*

8. During allergy season, my eyes become very dry and

   _____.
   insensitive-sensitive

9. _____ usually precedes a revolution.
   Dissent-Consent

10. Marcus accused his boss of being too demanding and

    _____.
    sensitive-insensitive

11. Being stung by a bee is not a pleasant _____.
    sensation-sentiment

12. When Lorena saw her straight-A report card, her

    _____ was one of extreme jubilation.
    consent-sentiment

Lesson 18–Prefixes, Roots, and Suffixes

Activity C
Choose the best word from the choice box below to complete each sentence and write it in the space.

> consent   sentiment   sensitive
> sensation   insensitive   dissent

1. When their pet hamster died, the _____ in the classroom was one of sadness.

2. Becky's skin is highly _____ to harsh detergents.

3. The judge gave his _____ to postpone the hearing.

4. When mom's foot fell asleep, she felt the _____ of pins and needles.

5. There was much _____ among the people when their right to vote was revoked.

6. Dad scolded my older brother for being so _____ when he hurt my feelings.

7. Grandpa's medications cause his skin to become very _____ to the sun.

8. Larry needed his parents' _____ to go on the field trip.

9. The main _____ throughout the election was one of intense anxiety.

10. I felt a tingling _____ up and down my left arm.

11. Vanessa's cold hands were _____ to the warmth of the fire.

12. Only one member of Congress expressed _____ over the ruling.

Lesson 18–Prefixes, Roots, and Suffixes

Activity D
Write a complete sentence for each word in the choice box below.

> consent   sentiment   sensitive
> sensation   insensitive   dissent

1. _____

   _____

2. _____

   _____

3. _____

   _____

4. _____

   _____

5. _____

   _____

6. _____

   _____

Show What You Know

REVIEW D

Draw a line from each word on the left to the correct meaning on the right.

1. plenty

2. import

3. inscribe

4. prediction

5. infertile

6. sensitive

7. transferable

8. reflex

9. diction

10. completion

a. relating to being not able to produce crops or offspring

b. the process or manner in which one speaks

c. tending to feel emotions and physical things easily

d. an automatic bending back away from something (like fire) or reacting to something (knee jerk)

e. to bring goods from a foreign source into a country

f. the state of having a full amount

g. the process of coming fully together to an expected end

h. a statement of what a person or group thinks will happen before it actually does

i. able to be carried across from one place to another

j. to write, print, or engrave words or letters into a surface

Show What You Know

REVIEW E
On each line circle the ONE word that is spelled correctly.

1. disent   dissent   discent

2. dictionary   dictionery   dictioniry

3. fertile   fertill   furtile

4. inflexable   inflexibile   inflexible

5. deplesion   depletion   dipletion

6. indescribable   indescribeable   undescribable

7. sentament   sentement   sentiment

8. reference   referance   referince

9. enflexible   inflexible   inflexable

10. cumplet   compleet   complete

Show What You Know

REVIEW F

Choose the best word from the choice box below to fill in the blanks. Use each word only once.

edict	consent	script	export
fertile		confer	deplete
inflexible	transportation		indescribable

1. The thief had time to _____ with his lawyer.

2. An illness can _____ the body of important vitamins.

3. The company arranged their _____ from the airport.

4. The government's _____ was followed.

5. Saul wrote the _____ for the school play.

6. The farmer used only _____ ground to plant his crops.

7. The _____ tree was damaged in the strong winds.

8. Brazil is known to _____ much of its coffee crop.

9. The flowers in the garden were of _____ beauty.

10. Jamie's parents gave their _____ for her to go.

Show What You Know

REVIEW G

Write a complete sentence for each word in the choice box below.

> plenty   reference   sensitive
>   import   reflection

1. _____

_____

_____

2. _____

_____

_____

3. _____

_____

_____

4. _____

_____

_____

5. _____

_____

_____

Lesson 19—Prefixes, Roots, and Suffixes

Prefix	Meaning
at-	to, toward
ex-	out, from, away
sub-	under, below

Root

tract

to draw or pull

Suffix	Meaning
-ion	an action or process
-or	one who, that which

Activity A

Underline the prefixes and suffixes and circle the roots in the choice box below. Then write the correct word for each definition.

> tractor   subtract attract
> attraction   extract   traction

1. To cause to draw towards oneself or itself, such as iron to a magnet: _____

2. To pull or draw out, such as a tooth: _____

3. To draw (take away) to make something below (less than) a larger unit, such as in math: _____

4. That which is used for pulling farm equipment behind it: _____

5. The action or process of pulling: _____

6. The act or process of drawing or pulling something towards oneself or itself: _____

Lesson 19–Prefixes, Roots, and Suffixes

Activity B

Write the correct word to complete the sentences below.

1. Mr. Benson used his _____ to pull our car from the ditch.
   traction-tractor

2. Mike's outgoing personality made it easy for him to

   _____ friends.
   attract-extract

3. Bryan learned how to _____ in kindergarten.
   subtract-extract

4. A farmer's _____ is a very essential piece of equipment.
   tractor-traction

5. The young couple had an instant _____ to one another.
   attraction-traction

6. It's easier to _____ using a calculator.
   extract-subtract

7. The movie star wore jeans and a sweatshirt hoping not to

   _____ attention.
   subtract-attract

8. The main _____ at the zoo was the koala bear.
   attraction-traction

9. The oral surgeon had to _____ the infected tooth.
   subtract-extract

10. Following the explosion, we had to _____ our Jeep from the pile of rubble.
    attract-extract

11. Due to the ski accident, the injured skier had his neck in

    _____ for six weeks.
    traction-attraction

12. Our truck's worn out tires had very little _____.
    attraction-traction

Lesson 19–Prefixes, Roots, and Suffixes

Activity C
Choose the best word from the choice box below to complete each sentence and write it in the space.

> tractor   subtract   attract
> attraction   extract   traction

1. Leroy painted his _____ bright red.

2. Jerry failed to _____ the cost of his gas.

3. It was easy for Roberto to _____ attention with his dyed green hair.

4. It was quite an _____ watching our new puppy Molly chase a grasshopper.

5. I love the taste of the juice I _____ from my garden vegetables.

6. When my car lost _____, it skidded off the road.

7. Mitch entered the _____ pull contest.

8. Janelle loves to multiply but hates to _____ in math.

9. The magnetic _____ of an object is affected by its mass.

10. Four wheel drives are designed to give vehicles better

    _____.

11. The construction worker used the claws of his hammer to

    _____ the nails from the board.

12. Their political rally was meant to _____ attention.

Lesson 19–Prefixes, Roots, and Suffixes

Activity D
Write a complete sentence for each word in the choice box below.

> tractor   subtract   attract
> attraction   extract   traction

1. _____

   _____

2. _____

   _____

3. _____

   _____

4. _____

   _____

5. _____

   _____

6. _____

   _____

Lesson 20–Prefixes, Roots, and Suffixes

Prefix	Meaning
con-	with, together
de-	from, away, down, apart
in-	in, into
in-	not
ob-	to, toward, against

Root

struct

to build

Suffix	Meaning
-ible	able to be
-ure	state, quality, act, that which

Activity A

Underline the prefixes and suffixes and circle the roots in the choice box below. Then write the correct word for each definition.

> indestructible   instruct   obstruct
> destruct   structure   construct

1. That which is built or erected: _____

2. To take apart, tear down, destroy: _____

3. To build by putting materials and parts together: _____

4. Not able to be taken apart or destroyed: _____

5. To build into someone's education information about a subject or how to do something: _____

6. To act against something being built or completed: _____

Lesson 20—Prefixes, Roots, and Suffixes

Activity B

Write the correct word to complete the sentences below.

1. Toys for toddlers should be as _____ as possible.
   destruct-indestructible

2. The king hired a private tutor to _____ his
   instruct-obstruct
   daughter.

3. The robot in the movie was able to self- _____.
   instruct-destruct

4. It took the workers two years to _____ the
   destruct-construct
   bridge.

5. A large _____ is being erected on the old
   structure-obstruct
   fairground site.

6. They removed the fallen tree so it wouldn't _____
   destruct-obstruct
   the road.

7. When a strong earthquake strikes, it's hard to find a structure
   that is totally _____.
   indestructible-obstruct

8. The _____ that the Indians lived in was made of
   construct-structure
   adobe.

9. The conscientious crossing guard always tried to
   _____ students on safety procedures.
   instruct-obstruct

10. Uncle Jack was unable to _____ the shed
    construct-destruct
    because some of the assembly parts were missing.

11. Our neighbor's house does not _____ our view of
    construct-obstruct
    the mountains.

12. In the old television series "Mission Impossible," the
    instructional tape at the beginning of the show would

    self- _____ within seconds.
    construct-destruct

Lesson 20–Prefixes, Roots, and Suffixes

Activity C
Choose the best word from the choice box below to complete each sentence and write it in the space.

> indestructible   instruct   obstruct
> destruct   structure   construct

1. The political leader's reputation was seemingly _____.

2. The professor used colorful charts to _____ the class.

3. The new _____ was shaped like a cylinder.

4. The device was set to self-_____ at a predetermined time.

5. The engineer designed a unique plan to _____ the tower.

6. The finance committee reported that lack of funds would

   _____ the building project.

7. The dilapidated building was an unsightly _____.

8. Contrary to public opinion at the time, the *Titanic* was not an

   _____ vessel.

9. Authorities found it necessary to _____ the passengers on customs regulations.

10. Chet could not _____ a sentence without the use of a metaphor.

11. The famous attorney vowed to never _____ justice.

12. It was a shock to see the missile self-_____ following its launching.

Lesson 20–Prefixes, Roots, and Suffixes

Activity D
Write a complete sentence for each word in the choice box below.

> indestructible   instruct   obstruct
> structure   construct   destruct

1. _____

_____

2. _____

_____

3. _____

_____

4. _____

_____

5. _____

_____

6. _____

_____

Lesson 21–Prefixes, Roots, and Suffixes

Prefix	Meaning
con-	with, together
re-	back, again

Root

vive

to live

Suffix	Meaning
-acious	having the quality of
-al	an action or process
i-al	like, related to
i-fy	to make, to act
-id	like, related to

Activity A

Underline the prefixes and suffixes and circle the roots in the choice box below. Then write the correct word for each definition.

revive   vivid   revival
vivacious   convivial   revivify

1. Related to lively and colorful images: _____

2. The process of bringing back life or interest in something: _____

3. To bring back to life or consciousness: _____

4. Having the quality of being lively (active, cheerful): _____

5. Related to being or living together in friendliness: _____

6. To make lively again: _____

Lesson 21–Prefixes, Roots, and Suffixes

Activity B

Write the correct word to complete the sentences below.

1. Adriana has a _____ imagination.
   convivial-vivid

2. The _____ girl makes a good cheerleader.
   vivacious-vivid

3. The paramedic used CPR to _____ the unconscious man.
   revive-convivial

4. At our annual reunion, we enjoyed the _____ of many family traditions.
   convivial-revival

5. The actress was known for her _____ nature.
   vivid-convivial

6. The upbeat music served to _____ the audience.
   revivify-revival

7. The old barn was painted a _____ red.
   vivid-vivacious

8. Brad's _____ disposition made him perfect for
   vivid-convivial

   the job of social director.

9. Dillon's _____ personality always helped to cheer
   vivacious-vivid

   up his friends.

10. A hot shower and a cup of tea will help _____
    revive-convivial
    you.

11. The documentary was about the _____ of the Old
    revival-vivid
    South following the Civil War.

12. The crisp mountain air helped to _____ my
    convivial-revivify
    spirits.

Lesson 21—Prefixes, Roots, and Suffixes

Activity C
Choose the best word from the choice box below to complete each sentence and write it in the space.

> revive   vivid   revival
> vivacious   convivial   revivify

1. The nurse used smelling salts to _____ my aunt.

2. It's fun to take a tour with such _____ people.

3. The artist used such bright and _____ colors.

4. Carmen feels so energized and _____ after her exercise class.

5. I learned important _____ techniques in my CPR class.

6. A leader with real charisma is needed to _____ the political party.

7. An economic _____ is sweeping the country.

8. The repertory company decided to _____ plays from thirty years ago.

9. The banquet was quite a _____ affair.

10. The trees were so _____ in their fall colors of red and gold.

11. Our gym teacher is so strong and _____.

12. To _____ an animal is to bring it back to life.

Lesson 21—Prefixes, Roots, and Suffixes

Activity D

Write a complete sentence for each word in the choice box below.

> revive   vivid   revival
> vivacious   convivial   revivify

1. _____

   _____

2. _____

   _____

3. _____

   _____

4. _____

   _____

5. _____

   _____

6. _____

   _____

Lesson 22—Prefixes, Roots, and Suffixes

Prefix	Meaning
con-	with, together
di-	apart
in-	in, into
re-	back, again

Root

vert, vers

to turn

Suffix	Meaning
-ible	able to be
-ical	like, related to
-ion	an action or process

Activity A

Underline the prefixes and suffixes, and circle the roots in the choice box below. Then, write the correct word for each definition.

> reversible   revert   vertical
> invert   convertible   diversion

1. Able to be turned back and again; inside out (such as a jacket): _____

2. Related to being turned in an upright position: _____

3. To turn inside out or upside down: _____

4. The process of moving apart or changing from a course or activity: _____

5. To turn back to a previous state: _____

6. Able to be one or more different ways or use (together in one item such as a sofa bed): _____

Lesson 22—Prefixes, Roots, and Suffixes

Activity B
Write the correct word to complete the sentences below.

1. Because the spell was _____, we were able to
   <u>reversible-vertical</u>
   turn the frog back into a prince.

2. We will _____ the river to its original path to the
   <u>invert-revert</u>
   ocean.

3. My aunt's sofa is _____ so people can use it as a
   <u>convertible-reversible</u>
   bed.

4. His favorite _____ from his homework is movies.
   <u>diversion-reversible</u>

5. Please _____ the catsup bottle so the catsup will
   <u>invert-revert</u>
   come out easier.

6. Football goal posts are always _____.
   <u>vertical-convertible</u>

7. If you _____ the order of Sue Nord's name, then
   <u>invert-revert</u>
   her name would be Nord Sue.

8. The comforter on the bed is _____.
   <u>reversible-convertible</u>

9. My uncle drives a black _____.
   <u>vertical-convertible</u>

10. A _____ line runs straight-up from the ground.
    <u>vertical-reversible</u>

11. The _____ from arguing with my sister was a
    <u>diversion-convertible</u>
    time out.

12. If you do not understand the answer, _____ to
    <u>revert-invert</u>
    the question.

Lesson 22—Prefixes, Roots, and Suffixes

Activity C
Choose the best word from the choice box below to complete each sentence and write it in the space.

> reversible   revert   vertical
> invert   convertible   diversion

1. A _____ jacket can also be worn inside out.

2. Tad will create a _____ so his sister can sneak up behind their mom and scare her.

3. My grandmother has to sleep with her head in a _____ position to help her breathe.

4. A transformer toy is a _____ toy because it transforms into other shapes.

5. Would it help to _____ to the previous lesson?

6. You can _____ an hourglass to keep track of time.

7. Beth wore her new _____ ski jacket yesterday.

8. If a plane rolls upside down, it will _____ passengers.

9. The _____ sofa makes a comfortable bed.

10. Faking the pass was just a _____, so we could run for a touchdown.

11. We will _____ to the old rules of the *Monopoly* game.

12. The _____ columns held the roof of the building up.

Lesson 22–Prefixes, Roots, and Suffixes

Activity D
Write a complete sentence for each word in the choice box below.

> reversible   revert   vertical
> invert   convertible   diversion

1. _____

_____

2. _____

_____

3. _____

_____

4. _____

_____

5. _____

_____

6. _____

_____

Lesson 23–Prefixes, Roots, and Suffixes

Prefix	Meaning
con-	with, together
pre-	before
re-	back, again
sub-	under, below

Root

serve

to serve, protect, save

Suffix	Meaning
-ant	one who, that which
-ation	an action or process
i-ent	like, related to

Activity A

Underline the prefixes and suffixes and circle the roots in the choice box below. Then write the correct word for each definition.

> preserve   reserve   servant
> conservation   subservient   preservation

1. To keep something back or save for future use (protect wetlands, buy tickets for an event): _____

2. One who is hired to serve: _____

3. The action of together protecting the use of natural resources such as gas and forests: _____

4. To protect the quality or condition of something before anything can harm it: _____

5. Related to serving under someone in authority: _____

6. The process of keeping something safe or protected before anything can harm it: _____

Lesson 23–Prefixes, Roots, and Suffixes

Activity B

Write the correct word to complete the sentences below.

1. We must all strive to _____ our natural resources.
   preserve-reserve

2. The mayor is a public _____.
   subservient-servant

3. The world will run out of oil unless it practices

   _____.
   conservation-preservation

4. A good leader's policies must be _____ to the
   needs of the people.   *subservient-servant*

5. If the public works at _____ of electricity,
   preservation-conservation

   blackouts might be avoided.

6. Ted decided to keep the equivalent of six months' earnings as

   a _____.
      reserve-preserve

7. His _____ behavior to his boss makes his fellow
      servant-subservient

   workers wince.

8. The park was established for the _____ of wildlife.
      preservation-reserve

9. You can have strawberries in winter if you _____
   them in the summer.   *reserve-preserve*

10. It's often wise to _____ judgment.
         preserve-reserve

11. Our butler, Thomas, is a kind and gracious _____.
            servant-subservient

12. The public is concerned about some of the chemicals used in

    food _____.
       conservation-preservation

Lesson 23–Prefixes, Roots, and Suffixes

Activity C
Choose the best word from the choice box below to complete each sentence and write it in the space.

> preserve   reserve   servant
> conservation   subservient   preservation

1. The old castle is in a poor state of _____.

2. The librarian has put the book on _____ for me.

3. The residents hope to _____ the character of their town while improving its appearance.

4. The new manager forced the workers to adopt a _____ position in the company.

5. Mark was a civil _____ for many years.

6. Energy _____ reduces fuel costs and helps the environment as well.

7. The government was accused of being _____ to the interests of special groups.

8. The wealthy man's _____ was very well paid.

9. The prime minister is committed to the _____ of his country's national interests.

10. Fran put varnish on the wood table to help _____ it.

11. Bob decided that the _____ of his energy might help him win the race.

12. I _____ Fridays for shopping and cleaning.

Lesson 23–Prefixes, Roots, and Suffixes

Activity D
Write a complete sentence for each word in the choice box below.

preserve   reserve   servant
conservation   preservation   subservient

1. _____

   _____

2. _____

   _____

3. _____

   _____

4. _____

   _____

5. _____

   _____

6. _____

   _____

Lesson 24—Roots and Suffixes

Root	Meaning
cline	to lean, bend, slope
meter	to measure
stat	to stay, position

Root

therm, thermos

heat

Suffix	Meaning
-al	like, related to

Activity A

The words in the choice box have been formed by combining the main root **therm**, **thermos** and additional roots: **clin**, **meter**, and **stat**. In one word, the suffix **-al** has been used.

Underline the suffix and circle the roots in the choice box. Then write each word at the end of its matching definition.

> thermos   thermal   thermometer
> thermostat   thermocline

1. A vacuum bottle used to keep heated drinks or soups hot: _____

2. Relating to or producing heat: _____

3. An instrument for measuring body temperature (for fever): _____

4. A layer of water between warm surface water and cold deep water (in a lake or bay) where the temperature changes abruptly: _____

5. An electric instrument that maintains indoor temperatures by starting or stopping the supply of heat: _____

Lesson 24–Roots and Suffixes

Activity B
Write the correct word to complete the sentences below.

1. Mom filled my _____ with hot apple cider.
   thermos-thermostat

2. Yellowstone National Park is known for its _____
   thermometer-thermal
   pools.

3. Our car is equipped with a _____ that indicates
   thermocline-thermometer
   both the inside and outside temperature.

4. We have a programmable _____ to control the
   thermostat-thermos
   temperature in our house.

5. The summer _____ in the lake disappears when
   thermometer-thermocline
   autumn storms churn and mix the water temperatures.

6. A _____ can keep things hot and it can keep things
   thermos-thermostat
   cold.

7. Some areas can tap into _____ energy.
   thermocline-thermal

8. The cover on our _____ was broken.
   thermostat-thermal

9. The divers were prepared for the cold water _____
   thermostat-thermocline
   layer as they dove deeper.

10. A digital _____ is safer than a mercury one.
    thermos-thermometer

Lesson 24–Roots and Suffixes

Activity C
Choose the best word from the choice box below to complete each sentence and write it in the space.

> thermos   thermal   thermometer
> thermostat   thermocline

1. On cold days, it's great to have a _____ of hot chocolate.

2. In Alaska almost everyone wears _____ underwear.

3. I can't believe the outside _____ read 105 degrees.

4. Dad turns the _____ down, then mom walks by and turns it up again.

5. It feels weird when you're swimming in a warm lake and suddenly feel the effects of a _____.

6. Dad takes a _____ of hot coffee to work with him each day.

7. Rather than an x-ray, the medical staff used _____ imaging on my knee.

8. Mom got the _____ to take my little brother's temperature.

9. We set the _____ at 70 degrees.

10. Some sea animals cannot cope with the sudden temperature changes a _____ brings.

Lesson 24–Roots and Suffixes

Activity D
Write a complete sentence for each word in the choice box below.

thermos   thermal   thermometer
thermostat   thermocline

1. _____

_____

_____

2. _____

_____

_____

3. _____

_____

_____

4. _____

_____

_____

5. _____

_____

_____

Show What You Know

REVIEW H

Draw a line from each word in the left column to its correct meaning.

1. destruct

2. thermal

3. preserve

4. attract

5. reversible

6. convivial

7. obstruct

8. thermometer

9. subservient

10. revivify

a. to protect the quality or condition of something before anything can harm it

b. able to be turned back and again; inside out (such as a jacket)

c. to prevent something from being built or completed

d. related to serving under someone in authority

e. related to or producing heat

f. an instrument for measuring body temperature (for fever)

g. to make lively again

h. to cause to draw towards oneself or itself, such as iron to a magnet

i. to take apart, tear down, destroy

j. related to being or living together in friendliness

Show What You Know

REVIEW I

On each line circle the ONE word that is spelled correctly.

1. indistructible   indestructible   indestructable

2. thermostat   thermastat   thermistat

3. subserrvint   subserviant   subservient

4. tracter   tracktor   tractor

5. convertible   convertable   convertoble

6. vivatious   vivacious   vivascious

7. perservation   presavation   preservation

8. divertion   diversion   divertsion

9. restructure   restructsure   restructer

10. servant   servent   servient

Show What You Know

REVIEW J

Choose the best word from the choice box below to complete the sentences. Use each word only once.

> thermos   conservation   vivid
> instruct   traction   vivacious
> revival   reserve   structure

1. The zoo believed in the importance of wildlife _____.

2. The new _____ stood 100 stories high.

3. His job was to _____ students in grammar.

4. She always packed a _____ of hot coffee for work.

5. Tony's broken leg had to be in _____ for six weeks.

6. The drama club staged a _____ of an old play.

7. Jalee was wearing the most _____ purple dress.

8. Dad called ahead to _____ our seats at the theater.

9. Keesha's _____ smile made her liked by everyone.

Show What You Know

REVIEW K

Write a complete sentence for each word in the choice box below.

restructure   revivify   diversion
attraction   subservient

1. _____

_____

_____

2. _____

_____

_____

3. _____

_____

_____

4. _____

_____

_____

5. _____

_____

_____

Answers

LESSON 1   Pages 1-3
Activity A   Page 1

microscope   periscope   telescope

Activity B   Page 2
1. peri(scop)e
2. tele(scop)e
3. micro(scop)e

Activity C   Pages 2-3
acrophobia, astronaut, thermometer, geography

Activity D   Page 3
1. Geography
2. thermometer
3. acrophobia
4. astronaut

LESSON 2   Pages 4-7
A   <u>unicorn</u>   has just a single horn.

Activity A   Page 5

re(cycle)

dis(agree)

dis(appear)

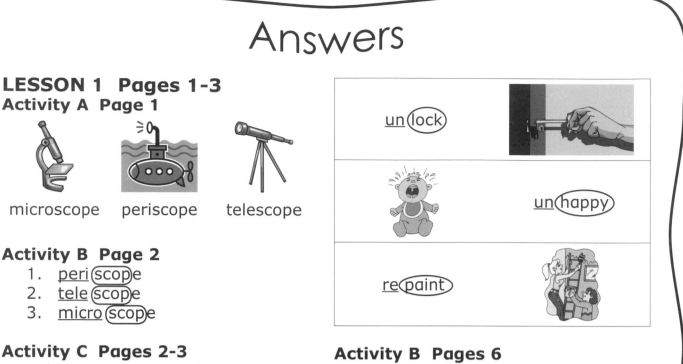

un(lock)

un(happy)

re(paint)

Activity B   Pages 6
<u>dis</u> appear = not there anymore; gone
<u>re</u> cycle = use again; reuse
<u>dis</u> agree = not agree
<u>un</u> happy = not happy
<u>re</u> paint = paint again; paint over
<u>un</u> lock = to open

Activity C   Page 7
1. re(cycle)
2. re(paint)
3. un(lock)
4. dis(agree)
5. un(happy)
6. dis(appear)
7. re(appear)

LESSON 3   Pages 8-10
Activity A   Page 8
1. A person or animal that is forcibly taken and kept.
2. One who works with medicines and drugs.
3. Having an idea that is moderate; at neither extreme.

Activity B Page 9

terrorist   terrorism

journalism   journalist

egoist   egoism

optimism   optimist

hypnotist   hypnotism

idealist   idealism

plagiarism   plagiarist

modernist   modernism

Activity C Page 10

(teach)er   (golf)er   (quiet)er
(teach)able   (accept)able   (quiet)ly
(dark)ness   (quiet)ness   (thought)ful

1. quietly
2. teachable
3. golfer
4. quietness
5. thoughtful
6. acceptable
7. darkness
8. quieter, teacher

LESSON 4 Pages 11-12
Activity A Page 11

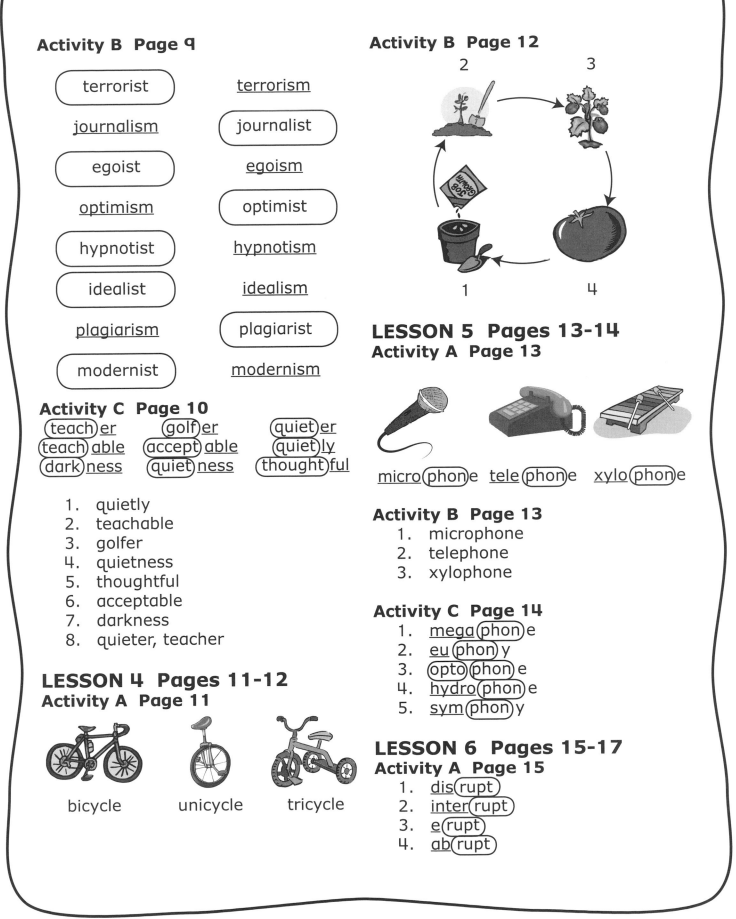

bicycle   unicycle   tricycle

Activity B Page 12

2   3

1   4

LESSON 5 Pages 13-14
Activity A Page 13

micro(phon)e   tele(phon)e   xylo(phon)e

Activity B Page 13
1. microphone
2. telephone
3. xylophone

Activity C Page 14
1. mega(phon)e
2. eu(phon)y
3. (opto)(phon)e
4. hydro(phon)e
5. sym(phon)y

LESSON 6 Pages 15-17
Activity A Page 15
1. dis(rupt)
2. inter(rupt)
3. e(rupt)
4. ab(rupt)

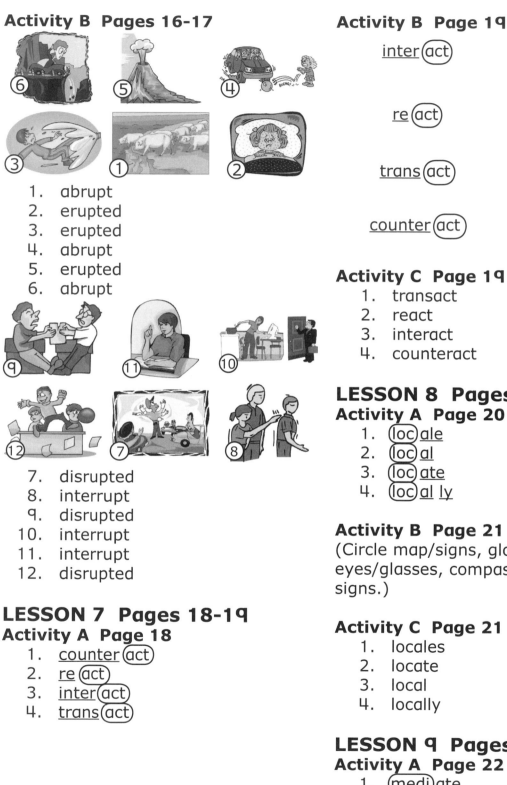

Activity B Pages 16-17

1. abrupt
2. erupted
3. erupted
4. abrupt
5. erupted
6. abrupt

7. disrupted
8. interrupt
9. disrupted
10. interrupt
11. interrupt
12. disrupted

LESSON 7 Pages 18-19
Activity A Page 18
1. counter (act)
2. re (act)
3. inter (act)
4. trans (act)

Activity B Page 19

inter (act)

re (act)

trans (act)

counter (act)

Activity C Page 19
1. transact
2. react
3. interact
4. counteract

LESSON 8 Pages 20-21
Activity A Page 20
1. (loc) ale
2. (loc) al
3. (loc) ate
4. (loc) al ly

Activity B Page 21
(Circle map/signs, globe, country map, eyes/glasses, compass, and local signs.)

Activity C Page 21
1. locales
2. locate
3. local
4. locally

LESSON 9 Pages 22-23
Activity A Page 22
1. (medi) ate
2. (medi) ator
3. (medi) um
4. (medi) an

Activity B Page 23

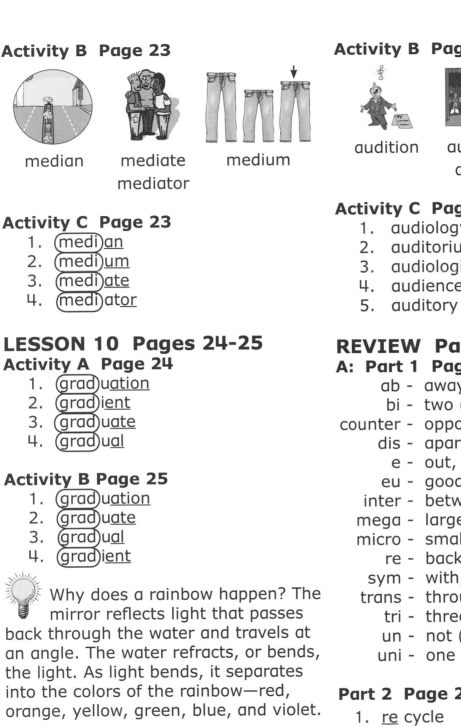

median   mediate   medium
              mediator

Activity C Page 23
1. (medi)an
2. (medi)um
3. (medi)ate
4. (medi)ator

LESSON 10 Pages 24-25
Activity A Page 24
1. (grad)uation
2. (grad)ient
3. (grad)uate
4. (grad)ual

Activity B Page 25
1. (grad)uation
2. (grad)uate
3. (grad)ual
4. (grad)ient

💡 Why does a rainbow happen? The mirror reflects light that passes back through the water and travels at an angle. The water refracts, or bends, the light. As light bends, it separates into the colors of the rainbow—red, orange, yellow, green, blue, and violet.

LESSON 11 Pages 26-27
Activity A Page 26
1. (audi)torium
2. (audi)ology
3. (audi)tion
4. (audi)olog ist
5. (audi)ence
6. (audi)tory

Activity B Page 27

audition   auditorium   audiologist
            audience

Activity C Page 27
1. audiology
2. auditorium
3. audiologist
4. audience
5. auditory

REVIEW Pages 28-32
A: Part 1 Page 28
ab - away, from (10)
bi - two (12)
counter - opposite, against (14)
dis - apart, opposite of (1)
e - out, away, from (3)
eu - good, well, pleasant (5)
inter - between, among (13)
mega - large, great (7)
micro - small (11)
re - back, again (2)
sym - with, together (9)
trans - through, across, beyond (6)
tri - three (15)
un - not (4)
uni - one (8)

Part 2 Page 29
1. re cycle
2. un lock
3. uni corn
4. dis agree
5. dis appear
6. inter act
7. mega phone
8. un happy
9. re paint
10. tri cycle
11. counter act
12. e rupt
13. sym phony
14. dis approve
15. micro scope

Part 3 Pages 30-31
Answers will vary.
1. recycle: to use or cycle again
2. unlock: to open
3. unicorn: one-horned animal
4. disagree: not agree
5. disappear: not there
6. interact: to be involved with others
7. megaphone: a cone-shaped device that makes a voice or sound louder
8. unhappy: not happy
9. repaint: paint again
10. tricycle: a three-wheeled mode of transportation
11. counteract: to do the opposite of
12. erupt: to emerge from something with great force
13. symphony: a variety of sounds played together
14. disapprove: not approve
15. microscope: a device for seeing small things much larger

B: Part 1 Page 32
1. medi <u>um</u>   5. gradi <u>ent</u>
2. gradu <u>ate</u>   6. mediat <u>or</u>
3. loc <u>ale</u>   7. audit <u>ion</u>
4. audit <u>orium</u>   8. loc <u>ate</u>

Part 2 Pages 32-33
Answers will vary.
1. medium: middle, half, average
2. graduate: one who completes steps or grades in high school or college
3. locale: a region
4. auditorium: large hall for performances, lectures, etc.
5. gradient: a blending of one color into another or steepness of a road

6. mediator: one who acts between two opposite sides to solve problems
7. audition: try out for
8. locate: find

C: Page 33

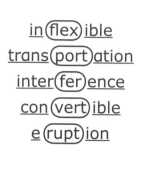

re(cycl)able   in(flex)ible
inter(act)ion   trans(port)ation
re(mov)able   inter(fer)ence
con(struct)ion   con(vert)ible
re(tract)able   e(rupt)ion
re(viv)al

LESSON 12 Pages 34-37
Activity A Page 34
1. (dict)ion <u>ary</u>
2. e(dict)
3. (dict)ion
4. pre(dict)ion
5. (dict)<u>ate</u>
6. pre(dict)

Activity B Page 35
1. prediction
2. diction
3. dictionary
4. edict
5. predict
6. dictate
7. diction
8. dictionary
9. edict
10. predict
11. prediction
12. dictate

Activity C Page 36
1. predict
2. diction
3. edict
4. dictate

5. diction
6. dictionary
7. prediction
8. predict
9. dictate
10. edict
11. dictionary
12. prediction

Activity D Page 37
Sentences will vary.

LESSON 13 Pages 38-41
Activity A Page 38
1. (fert)ile
2. trans(fer)
3. re(fer)ence
4. con(fer)
5. in(fer)til e
6. trans(fer)able

Activity B Page 39
1. confer
2. reference
3. transferable
4. fertile
5. transfer
6. confer
7. fertile
8. reference
9. infertile
10. transfer
11. infertile
12. transferable

Activity C Page 40
1. confer
2. fertile
3. transfer
4. reference
5. transferable
6. infertile
7. confer
8. transfer

9. transferable
10. fertile
11. reference
12. infertile

Activity D Page 41
Sentences will vary.

LESSON 14 Pages 42-45
Activity A Page 42
1. (flex) or
2. re (flect) ion
3. in (flex) ible
4. re (flex)
5. (flex) ible

Activity B Page 43
1. inflexible
2. flexor
3. Flexible
4. reflection
5. reflex
6. reflection
7. flexor
8. flexible
9. reflex
10. inflexible

Activity C Page 44
1. reflection
2. flexible
3. inflexible
4. flexor
5. reflex
6. inflexible
7. flexible
8. reflection
9. flexor
10. reflex

Activity D Page 45
Sentences will vary.

LESSON 15 Pages 46-49
Activity A Page 46
1. trans(port)ation
2. im(port)
3. (port)able
4. ex(port)
5. sup(port)

Activity B Page 47
1. export
2. support
3. import
4. transportation
5. portable
6. export
7. support
8. import
9. transportation
10. portable

Activity C Page 48
1. import
2. support
3. export
4. transportation
5. support
6. portable
7. import
8. portable
9. export
10. transportation

Activity D Page 49
Sentences will vary.

LESSON 16 Pages 50-53
Activity A Page 50
1. com(plet)ion
2. de(plet)e
3. com(plet)e
4. (plen)ty
5. de(plet)ion

Activity B Page 51
1. plenty
2. deplete
3. completion
4. complete
5. depletion
6. completion
7. deplete
8. plenty
9. complete
10. depletion

Activity C Page 52
1. plenty
2. depletion
3. complete
4. deplete
5. completion
6. depletion
7. plenty
8. completion
9. deplete
10. complete

Activity D Page 53
Sentences will vary.

LESSON 17 Pages 54-57
Activity A Page 54
1. in de(scrib)able
2. (script)
3. de(scrib)e
4. in(scrib)e
5. de(script)ive
6. in(script)ion

Activity B Page 55
1. inscription
2. indescribable
3. script
4. describe
5. inscription
6. indescribable
7. descriptive
8. script
9. inscribe
10. Describe
11. descriptive
12. inscribe

Activity C Page 56
1. indescribable
2. inscription
3. script
4. inscribe
5. descriptive
6. describe
7. inscription
8. indescribable
9. script
10. inscribe
11. describe
12. descriptive

Activity D Page 57
Sentences will vary.

LESSON 18 Pages 58-61
Activity A Page 58
1. (sens)itive
2. con(sent)
3. (sent)iment
4. in(sens)itive
5. dis(sent)
6. (sens)ation

Activity B Page 59
1. consent
2. sentiment
3. sensitive

4. sensation
5. insensitive
6. dissent
7. consent
8. sensitive
9. Dissent
10. insensitive
11. sensation
12. sentiment

Activity C Page 60
1. sentiment
2. sensitive
3. consent
4. sensation
5. dissent
6. insensitive
7. sensitive
8. consent
9. sentiment
10. sensation
11. insensitive
12. dissent

Activity D Page 61
Sentences will vary.

REVIEW Pages 62-65
D: Part 1 Page 62
1. f		6. c
2. e		7. i
3. j		8. d
4. h		9. b
5. a		10. g

E: Page 63
1. dissent	6. indescribable
2. dictionary	7. sentiment
3. fertile	8. reference
4. flexibility	9. inflexible
5. depletion	10. complete

F: Page 64
1. confer
2. deplete
3. transportation
4. edict
5. script
6. fertile
7. flexibility
8. export
9. indescribable
10. consent

G: Page 65
Sentences will vary.

LESSON 19 Pages 66-69
Activity A Page 66
1. at(tract)
2. ex(tract)
3. sub(tract)
4. (tract)or
5. (tract)ion
6. at(tract)ion

Activity B Page 67
1. tractor
2. attract
3. subtract
4. tractor
5. attraction
6. subtract
7. attract
8. attraction
9. extract
10. extract
11. traction
12. traction

Activity C Page 68
1. tractor
2. subtract
3. attract
4. attraction
5. extract

6. traction
7. tractor
8. subtract
9. attraction
10. traction
11. extract
12. attract

Activity D Page 69
Sentences will vary.

LESSON 20 Pages 70-73
Activity A Page 70
1. (struct)ure
2. de(struct)
3. con(struct)
4. in de(struct)ible
5. in(struct)
6. ob(struct)

Activity B Page 71
1. indestructible
2. instruct
3. destruct
4. construct
5. structure
6. obstruct
7. indestructible
8. structure
9. instruct
10. construct
11. obstruct
12. destruct

Activity C Page 72
1. indestructible
2. instruct
3. structure
4. destruct
5. construct
6. obstruct
7. structure
8. indestructible
9. instruct

10. construct
11. obstruct
12. destruct

Activity D Page 73
Sentences will vary.

LESSON 21 Pages 74-77
Activity A Page 74
1. (viv)id
2. re (viv) al
3. re (viv)e
4. (viv) acious
5. con (viv)i al
6. re (viv)i fy

Activity B Page 75
1. vivid
2. vivacious
3. revive
4. revival
5. convivial
6. revivify
7. vivid
8. convivial
9. vivacious
10. revive
11. revival
12. revivify

Activity C Page 76
1. revive
2. convivial
3. vivid
4. vivacious
5. revival
6. revivify
7. revival
8. revive
9. convivial
10. vivid
11. vivacious
12. revivify

Activity D Page 77
Sentences will vary.

LESSON 22 Pages 78-81
Activity A Page 78
1. re (vers) ible
2. (vert) ical
3. in (vert)
4. di (vers) ion
5. re (vert)
6. con (vert) ible

Activity B Page 79
1. reversible
2. revert
3. convertible
4. diversion
5. invert
6. vertical
7. invert
8. reversible
9. convertible
10. vertical
11. diversion
12. revert

Activity C Page 80
1. reversible
2. diversion
3. vertical
4. convertible
5. revert
6. invert
7. reversible
8. invert
9. convertible
10. diversion
11. revert
12. vertical

Activity D Page 81
Sentences will vary.

LESSON 23 Pages 82-85
Activity A Page 82
1. re(serve)
2. (serv)ant
3. con(serv)ation
4. pre(serve)
5. sub(serv)i ent
6. pre(serv)ation

Activity B Page 83
1. preserve
2. servant
3. conservation
4. subservient
5. conservation
6. reserve
7. subservient
8. preservation
9. preserve
10. reserve
11. servant
12. preservation

Activity C Page 84
1. preservation
2. reserve
3. preserve
4. subservient
5. servant
6. conservation
7. subservient
8. servant
9. preservation
10. preserve
11. conservation
12. reserve

Activity D Page 85
Sentences will vary.

LESSON 24 Pages 86-89
Activity A Page 86
1. (thermo)s
2. (therm)al
3. (thermo)meter
4. (thermo)cline
5. (thermo)stat

Activity B Page 87
1. thermos
2. thermal
3. thermometer
4. thermostat
5. thermocline
6. thermos
7. thermal
8. thermostat
9. thermocline
10. thermometer

Activity C Page 88
1. thermos
2. thermal
3. thermometer
4. thermostat
5. thermocline
6. thermos
7. thermal
8. thermometer
9. thermostat
10. thermocline

Activity D Page 89
Sentences will vary.

REVIEW Pages 90-93
H: Page 90
1. i
2. e
3. a
4. h
5. b
6. j
7. c
8. f
9. d
10. g

I: Page 91
1. indestructible
2. thermostat
3. subservient
4. tractor
5. convertible
6. vivacious
7. preservation
8. diversion
9. restructure
10. servant

J: Page 92
1. conservation
2. structure
3. instruct
4. thermos
5. traction
6. revival
7. vivid
8. reserve
9. vivacious

K: Page 93
Sentences will vary.